JOYCE HUGGETT

Walking with Jesus

A reflective group study course
for Lent to Easter

**kevin
mayhew**

The publishers wish to express their gratitude to the following for permission to include copyright material in this book:

Ronnie Barclay for the quotation by William Barclay from *The Daily Study Bible: The Gospel of Luke* (The Saint Andrew Press, 1958).

Mother Raphaela (www.holymyrrhbearers.com) for the extract from *The Lenten Triodion*.

SPCK, Holy Trinity Church, Marylebone Road, London, NW1 4DU, for the extracts from *Sensing the Passion* by Kevin Scully (SPCK/Triangle, 1997) and the prayer 'Holy, holy, holy', taken from *All Desires Known* by Janet Morley (SPCK, 1992).

Bible quotations (where indicated) are taken from *The Message* © Copyright Eugene H. Peterson, 1993, 1994, 1995. Used by permission of NavPress Publishing Group.

All other Bible quotations are taken from The Good News Bible, published by The Bible Societies/HarperCollins Publishers Ltd., UK. © American Bible Society, 1966, 1971, 1976, 1992.

First published in 2002 by
KEVIN MAYHEW LTD
Buxhall, Stowmarket, Suffolk IP14 3BW
E-mail: info@kevinmayhewltd.com

© 2002 Joyce Huggett

9 8 7 6 5 4 3 2

ISBN 1 84003 987 6
Catalogue No. 1500548

Cover design by Angela Selfe
Edited by Elisabeth Bates
Typeset by Louise Selfe

Printed and bound in Great Britain

*For Margaret
For years of friendship, encouragement,
mentoring and partnership through your artwork,
very warm thanks*

Contents

Acknowledgements

On the last page of my Advent book, *Waiting and Watching*, I suggested that groups using that book should pray that, as God had prepared them to celebrate Advent, now he would prepare them to journey through Lent and on into Easter.

As I wrote those words, I detected within myself a longing to suggest to groups ways in which they might engage creatively with material that would encourage them to take a fresh look at Jesus' suffering, death and resurrection. I mentioned this desire to no one but, several weeks later, Kevin Mayhew wrote to me inviting me to write this Lenten book. I found it impossible to say 'No'!

When I agreed to write the book, I had never met Kevin Mayhew or any of his team. While the book was being born, though, I spent a most enjoyable day in Suffolk visiting the Kevin Mayhew offices in their picturesque surroundings. There I was introduced to almost every member of the team. The welcome I received was so warm that, instead of singling out any individuals, I would like to thank the entire *team* for the encouragement and affirmation they gave me during that visit and for the friendly e-mails they have sent me since.

I should also like to thank my husband, David, for making time to read each section of the booklet as it evolved and for making kind but astute comments that enabled me to refine what I had first written.

In addition to David's encouragement, I had the support of many people whose love and prayers mean more to me and to my ministry than words can convey. To each of you *and* to my two artist friends I say a warm and heartfelt thank-you. Sr Elizabeth Ruth Obbard illustrated the footwashing on page 28 and drew the cockerel on page 56, while Sr Theresa Margaret's picture meditations appear on pages 38, 65, 79 and 83.

Introduction

'What are you going to give up for Lent?' That was a question my mother used to ask me each year as 'Pancake Day' drew near. My answer was always the same, 'Sweets'. I never understood *why* I should give up sweets for six weeks of the year, but the response always seemed to earn my mother's approval. It also earned me the reward of an Easter egg when Easter Sunday dawned so I was content with this nod in the direction of a Lenten fast.

In the early 1970s, though, I found myself fascinated by the historical roots of this custom of fasting throughout Lent. It was then that I discovered that, in the early Church, the six weeks that bridge 'Pancake Day' and Easter Sunday used to play a particularly significant part in the life of new converts to Christianity. Because Easter Sunday was considered the most important festival in the Church's year, it was the day earmarked for the baptism of such new believers. Before they could be baptised, though, they were required to attend preparation classes. On Pancake Day, they enrolled for these classes, then, every day during Lent, they attended seminars where they studied the Bible and the basics of the Christian faith.

The climax came on Easter Day when they made their baptismal vows and were received into the Church. On that day, they were allowed to pray the Lord's Prayer for the very first time.

This prolonged period of preparation became so obviously beneficial to new believers that other Christians began to sense the wisdom of using this six-week period to prepare for the Church's greatest celebration – Easter Day: the day Jesus rose from the dead.

For many years, this worked well. Gradually, though, the emphasis of the teaching changed. Instead of using these weeks to focus on the nature of God's love and acceptance, the stress seemed to be placed on one word, 'Don't'. So Lent became a time when Christians gave up things they really enjoy – like sweets or chocolate.

As often happens, when a pendulum swings too far in one direction, it swings back again so, during the 1960s, Christians were challenged to *give* during Lent. 'As well as giving up sweets, give the money you save to the poor . . .' the teaching insisted.

Were Christians tiring of these demands and counter-demands, I wonder?

Or were many of us yearning for something deeper as the 1970s dawned? I cannot speak for anyone else. I *can* speak for myself. As Lent began, I became aware that I was being wooed into the wilderness with Jesus. I read about his experiences, prayed with them and tried to discern what implications they had for my own life. As Lent wore on, and the days leading up to Good Friday drew near, I felt drawn to ponder Jesus' last journey to Jerusalem and the events that evolved as a result of that journey. Consequently, my love for Jesus deepened and my life was enriched in such a way that Easter Day became more and more meaningful as the years came and went.

Over a period of time, I accepted invitations to lead retreats during Lent and was moved to see and sense the way God's Spirit used these occasions to open retreatants' hearts to receive more and more of God's love. Then, in 1993, my husband and I went to live on the island of Cyprus.

We knew of no retreat centre on the island where we could hold retreats but, as our first Lent drew near, friends of ours agreed to allow us the exclusive use of their newly furbished hotel for an Easter retreat. There a retreat evolved that was different from any we had ever led before.

We were working for a missionary organisation at the time, so we invited our prayer supporters to visit the island. Those who came valued the opportunity to see where we were living. Even more, we all appreciated this opportunity to contemplate the mysteries of Holy Week together as well as to relish the wonder of Easter Day with one another.

Little did my husband and I realise, as we planned this retreat, that it was to be the beginning of an important new era for us. In the years that followed, we were privileged to lead many such events both in Cyprus, whose landscape is so reminiscent of the land where Jesus lived and died and rose again, and in neighbouring countries. Now, wherever I am at Eastertime, such vivid memories of those retreats surface that I am forced to recall the value of using more than our *minds* when we contemplate the mysteries that surround the life and ministry, the death and resurrection of Jesus. I say 'more than our minds' because those retreats convinced us that, when we engage our *senses* as well as our minds, whole new vistas open up for us. Kevin Scully puts the situation succinctly:

> The importance of the senses in the passion of Jesus is vital. They link us to him. His experiences were complete human experiences. His senses were complete human senses. His sight was like our sight.

His hearing was like our hearing. His touch was like our touch. His sense of smell was like ours. His taste was like our taste.[1]

In those days, we knew little about the insights neuropsychologists have so helpfully spelled out: that the human brain has two hemispheres and that these two sides respond to the stimuli they receive in remarkably different ways. While the left side of the brain responds with words that express rational judgements and logical analysis, the right side of the brain engages the emotions in its response. Very frequently this emotional response will use, too, the language of the visual as well as or rather than the verbal.

Although we knew little of the theory, we found ourselves entering into the fullness of both approaches to the part of the Gospel narrative Christians focus on during Holy Week. It happened in this way.

Easter retreats in Cyprus

After that first retreat, we decided to base our Lent retreats on our own home. Each retreat began on the Thursday before Easter: Maundy Thursday. Retreatants would arrive during the afternoon so that we could all share the evening meal together – just as, on the Thursday before he died, Jesus and his disciples shared together in what is now known as The Last Supper. As we ate, we would pause from time to time to read and ponder the mysteries that unfolded during that first 'Last Supper'.

The room where we ate together looked down on a valley that was studded with vineyards and olive groves. It was so like the Kidron Valley across which Jesus and his disciples walked when their celebratory meal was finished that, at the end of *our* meal, we would walk, in convoy, the length of our valley. There was no need for torches. By the time our silent walk began, the full moon had risen. Now it was bathing the entire neighbourhood in its eerie, silvery light. By the light of this moon and the myriad of stars that studded the velvet black sky, we walked past the vineyards and the ancient, gnarled olive trees, past the tiny Orthodox Church near our home and into the tranquillity and beauty of our small garden. There, in the deep-down stillness of the night, to the accompaniment of the chorus of the cicadas, we read the Gospel writers' accounts of Jesus' anguish in *his* garden – the Garden of Gethsemane. Then we would fall silent again as we listened to music like the hauntingly

---

1. Kevin Scully, *Sensing the Passion* (London, SPCK, Triangle, 1997), p. 2.

beautiful Taizé chant 'Stay here and keep watch with me' or songs from Adrian Snell's powerful musical *The Passion*. There, in the hiddenness of the garden and the wonder of the balmy night air we would each silently ponder the mystery of Christ's agony in the Garden of Gethsemane as we feasted on that rich cocktail: a mixture of listening to and meditating on Scripture, engaging in personal and private prayer, savouring music, poetry and the sounds of silence – as well as our own thoughts and insights.

Retreatants lingered late into the night, each leaving when they were ready regardless of what any of the others were doing or thinking – some staying late into the night.

Good Friday

Next morning, Good Friday, we would meet again, focusing, this time, on other aspects of the Gospel narrative: Jesus' trial, the flogging and so on. Again we used pictures, music and silence as well as words and discussion to enable us to engage with the mystery of our redemption, not only with our minds but with our whole being.

Just before midday, though, we would move to a different location. Near our home was a cave that was not unlike the kind of tomb where Jesus was probably buried. Facing the cave was a crop of rocks where people could sit and gaze into the tomb's yawning mouth. Just before noon, we would meet at the far end of the path that leads to this cave. There we would make a cross by placing on the ground two planks of wood, a hammer and some large nails. We would then invite retreatants to hammer in the nails that would fix the cross-beam to the larger piece of wood. Some people recoiled from the suggestion that they should hammer in the nails. Others found that the act of making that cross became a powerful part of their meditation on the events that resulted in the crucifixion of Jesus.

When the life-sized cross had been created, we would walk slowly and silently along the path. One by one, those who felt the urge took it in turns to carry the cross along the dusty path with its ruts and rocks that needed to be negotiated. At intervals, we would stop in the searing heat to read and reflect on relevant passages of Scripture and to listen to Good Friday hymns or other relevant Passiontide music. When, eventually, we reached the tomb, we watched while my husband carried the cross to the hill above the cave where he erected it and where it stood for the whole afternoon. For three hours, we would then sit in silence gazing from the cross to the cave and back again as we remembered the agony and death of Jesus.

The three-hour silence was punctuated by the reading aloud of relevant Scripture passages and the playing of other pieces of poignant music like, 'Were you there when they crucified my Lord?', 'Jesus, remember me when you come into your Kingdom', 'When I survey the wondrous cross'.

During this three-hour vigil, too, we reflected on our lives, asking ourselves,

'Is there anything that I would like to leave at the foot of Christ's cross as I contemplate him hanging there for me?'

When we discovered attitudes and thoughts, behaviour patterns and habits and other stumbling blocks that we felt we wanted to leave at the cross, we would wander away from the group and search for a stone that, by its size and shape, seemed to symbolise whatever it was that we wanted to relinquish. Later, as we sat together as a group again, those who felt they wanted to climbed the hill on which the cross had been erected. There, at the foot of the cross, we would lay the stones that represented our failures and shortcomings.

At the end of the three-hour vigil, we would watch my husband climb that same hill, gather up the stones, carry them to a pool near the cave and drop them into the water as he read Isaiah 53:

He was pierced for our transgressions,
he was crushed for our iniquities;
the punishment that brought us peace was upon him,
and by his wounds we are healed.
Isaiah 53:5 (NIV)

At the end of the vigil, some people would wander back to the place where they were staying. Others lingered near the cave. For all of us it had become holy ground. Some even returned on the Saturday – to listen to the sound of the sea lapping the shore, to feast on the sight of the empty cross, to imagine how it had felt for John and Mary to witness the burial of Jesus – and to anticipate the Day of Resurrection.

Easter Day

On Easter Day, just as the Marys in the Gospels made their way to the tomb 'while it was still dark' (John 20:1), so, in the darkness, *we* made *our* way to 'our' tomb. Once again, we met at the beginning of the path that led to the cave. Some carried torches, others depended on the light of the moon to help them pick their way through the potholes that peppered the path. We always walked in silence: listening to the tide tugging at the pebbles, wondering what we would see and sense and hear and experience and feel as we waited for the sun to rise. Some carried wild flowers, I always carried a portable, battery-operated cassette player!

When, eventually, we arrived at the entrance to the now-familiar cave, we stood in silence, remembering the agony of Good Friday and all that we had seen and sensed and heard and thought and felt and done on this spot on that day. We also watched the sky earnestly and expectantly as dawn slowly pushed back the dark of night.

As the light of dawn gradually edged away the darkness we watched – on tiptoe – for the first sign of sunrise. As soon as we glimpsed the first hint that the golden ball was sliding over the horizon, I pressed the 'play' button on the cassette player and we would thrill to the sounds of Handel's aria: 'I know that my Redeemer liveth.' That underlined the amazing news that Jesus did, in fact, rise from the dead. As the sun beamed a path of gold across the sea and while the birds chanted their dawn chorus, there, by the mouth of the empty cave, we would worship together in a service of Holy Communion and, like countless Christians throughout the world, we would renew our baptismal vows.

When we could tear ourselves away, we would walk to the hotel I mentioned earlier where we would dance an Israeli dance to express our joy further before tucking into an Easter breakfast that included chocolate Easter eggs!

Using our senses

Whenever I return to Cyprus, I visit 'our cave'. For me, it will always be holy ground; the place where so many of us were encountered by the Crucified, Risen Christ. For me, too, it became a place where, without even making a mental note of it at the time, I learned to engage the whole of my being in the contemplation of Christ:

- *my mind* as I read and pondered certain Bible passages
- *my imagination* as I felt the weight of the cross and carried it in the

sizzling heat of the noonday sun and as I pictured Jesus being hoisted onto his cross

- *my ears* as I 'heard' Christ cry out from the cross, 'heard' the wails and screams and cries and jibes of the crowd that gathered at the scene of Christ's crucifixion
- *my heart* as I searched it for attitudes and feelings that needed to be confessed and cast from me
- *my eyes* as they gazed from the cruel cross to the open-mouthed cave
- *my emotions* as I slipped myself into the sandals of the mother of Jesus as she stood watching her Son die or as I muttered to myself the phrase: *'He did it for me'*
- *my body* as I climbed the hill to the cross carrying my stones, as I knelt at the mouth of the cave, or as I danced as Easter Day dawned.
- *my innermost being* as it was touched by music and poetry and prayers

Walking with Jesus

Could Holy Week and Easter ever be the same when we returned to England, I wondered. I need not have worried. I have now been back in the homeland for more than four years and have found that God speaks as eloquently and powerfully in this country as in terrain that resembles the land in which Jesus lived. The secret is not geography or typography or even theology. The secret is to recognise that, at this special time of year, we are contemplating deep and life-changing mysteries.

A mystery, according to writers of both Old and New Testaments, is a hidden depth of the Christian faith that stretches beyond the reach of human reason.[1]

If the meaning of a mystery is to be revealed rather than concealed it must be contemplated, not simply with the human mind, but by engaging every part of our being: heart as well as head, imagination as well as logic, the visual as well as the verbal. Alister McGrath puts the situation powerfully when he reminds us that some of us will find ourselves excited by the logical analysis of the ideas of Scripture that are traditionally associated with systematic theology. Others, on the other hand, will find themselves so moved by the Bible's visual imagery that they may feel inspired to respond to the emotional impact it has made on them

---

1. A definition provided by Alister McGrath in *Knowing Christ* (London, Hodder and Stoughton, 2001), p. 26.

with colour or pictures, poetry or prose – perhaps in the form of a journal. One method is not more important or valid than another. Both are authentic and acceptable to God. Every Christian needs to beware of falling into the trap of believing that the way she or he views logic is the *only* way – the *right* way. As Alister McGrath rightly emphasises, Jesus does not want us merely to accumulate facts about him. He wants to befriend us, to embrace us, to enfold us in his arms. He longs that we should come to know him as a friend as well as our Saviour and Lord.[1]

It follows that, when a group of people meet together to feast on mystery, different members of the group will approach the material in different ways. Some will crave for the stillness in which they can pause to think before they speak. Others will appreciate the spontaneity of the kind of discussion where they can express their thoughts and views and experiences. The differences can feel frightening and result in divisiveness. They can also be enriching. It all depends on how they are handled and whether the needs of different personalities are recognised and met. For this reason, as in my earlier book, *Waiting and Watching*, I have structured each week's material in a particular way.

Each week, the pattern will be the same:

- First, the leader or another member of the group will help everyone to 'dial down' – to open themselves to receive whatever gift God has prepared for them. I have called this section **Group preparation**, and imagine that, most weeks, this could take in the region of ten minutes.

- The theme of the week will then be explored by focusing on a passage of Scripture – a section that I have called **Scripture focus**. This section may take a little longer than the first, depending on the length of the Bible passage chosen and the length of the comment that comes with it. The time span will normally take some fifteen minutes.

- After the Scripture focus, there are sections called **Personal exploration** and **Personal sharing**. The personal exploration section is intended to give each individual between ten and fifteen minutes to explore and respond to the Bible passage *on their own*. At the end of that time the group moves into personal sharing. During this personal sharing time, anyone who would like to is given a brief opportunity to share with others some of the insights that have come to them during this

---

1. Here I am building on insights expressed by Alister McGrath in *Knowing Christ* (London, Hodder & Stoughton, 2001), pp. 23, 28, 29.

time of reflection. Different people will take varying lengths of time when sharing in this way so the leader of the group will need to keep a careful eye on the clock and decide, and let group members know beforehand, how much time will be allocated to this important and moving part of the meeting.

The person who leads this part of the meeting may also need to remind the group that the aim of personal sharing is *not* to open up a discussion. It is simply to provide those who would value it with a chance to say, 'This is what I saw . . .', 'This is what I sensed . . .', 'This is what I heard . . .', 'This is what I experienced . . .' The role of the group is to listen with care and interest and to receive what is being expressed with no hint of judgement or expressed criticism. The group should be given no invitation to comment, except, perhaps, to say thank you to those who have plucked up courage to divulge the fruit of their meditation. Indeed, a powerful way of responding to such sharing is to suggest that, after each person has spoken, the group should remain silent for a few seconds – to ponder, to receive, to reflect, or to pray silently. Not everyone will want to voice the fruit of their pondering so no pressure should be put on anyone to participate verbally.

- **Group discussion** is scheduled to follow the sharing. Again, the group leader (in consultation with the group) will be the one who decides what proportion of the meeting will be given over to this. For some members of the group, it will be a vital part of the meeting. For others, the personal exploration and personal sharing mentioned above will prove to be more valuable. So, perhaps, most groups should aim at a maximum of twenty minutes for this section of the time together. During this discussion time, too, it needs to be remembered that we are not there to ciriticise one another but rather to *learn from* one another; to build one another up.

- The meeting ends with an invitation to gather up the thoughts and experiences of the time together by listening to music (possibly by candlelight) as well as the opportunity to pray together. I have called this final section **Worship time**, and envisage it taking between ten and fifteen minutes.

The group leader

You will notice that I have referred several times to 'the group leader'. The material has been arranged in such a way, though, that it would be possible, and probably advisable, for different people to lead different sections of the meeting. Some people, for example, are gifted in leading others into silence and reflection and quiet worship, while others have a gift for reading a Scripture passage aloud in such a way that the Bible really comes alive. Yet others have the kind of sensitivity that encourages group members to share the insights that have come to the surface for them during a period of reflection, while some are more skilled at leading a discussion. If you have been meeting regularly as a group before Lent begins, you will probably already know which people could best lead which parts of the meeting. If you are meeting together for the first time, you will have a more challenging task discerning who will best lead which section. It is possible that the quiet, retiring people who believe they are no good at leading *anything* will, in fact, excel at leading the group into stillness and encouraging group members to share the insights that have come to them during periods of reflection. When deciding who should lead which section of the meeting, it will be important to avoid the belief that *everyone* should be given a leadership role. Some of us are gifted in this way. Others are not.

A variety of groups

While writing this book, I have assumed that each group member will own their own copy. This way everyone can read and ponder the week's 'programme' before they come to the meeting, during the meeting itself and when they return home. Some may even want to reflect further on each week's material in their own time of quiet at home – recalling what has been said and felt and learned during group times.

While I have been writing these reflections, I have had a number of groups in mind: church house groups who are looking for material written especially for the eight-week period leading up to and including Easter; groups that have been convened especially for this period of time – especially ecumenical groups that bring together Christians from two or more denominations; groups of young mums whose baby-minding needs have been kindly catered for by friends, family or church members – and so on.

Many Lent groups meet only during the weeks leading up to Holy Week. As I wrote, though, it seemed right to include material for Holy Week itself and to suggest that, if at all possible, the group should meet at least once *after* Easter to celebrate the greatest mystery of all: that Jesus did not remain in the tomb. He rose again and returned to his friends – albeit bringing a mixture of joy and bewilderment.

Further reading

Over the years, a huge number of books have been written to help us to fathom the depths of the meaning of the mystery that enshrouds the suffering, death and resurrection of Jesus. One that I read every Lent is *The Day Christ Died* by Jim Bishop.[1] This book was out of print for many years but was recently brought back into circulation and I recommend it as background reading for those who would like to engage deeply with the material in *Walking With Jesus*.

Music

Many people find that music plays an important part in their attempt to walk closely with Jesus. Each week, I have suggested specific hymns or songs or choruses or chants that could helpfully be played and I have indicated where these particular tracks may be found. If these pieces of music are not available to the group for any reason, other songs or chants, choruses or hymns could be used as substitutes. In fact, members of groups might enjoy bringing to the group music that is especially meaningful for them during this very special time of the Church's year.

My prayer

My prayer, as this book goes to print, is that each group using it may be so flexible that each group member may grow in their knowledge and love of Jesus and that, as a result, they may gradually grasp the fact that God loves them uniquely and unconditionally. I pray, too, that this assurance will prompt them to love him more deeply and become more like him as Easter Sunday dawns – and beyond.

JOYCE HUGGETT

---

1. Jim Bishop, *The Day Christ Died* (London, Hodder and Stoughton, 1999).

Week 1

In the desert

Thomas Merton once claimed that Lent is a time for special reflection. It can be a forty-day retreat when each Christian, by prayer and fasting, attempts to walk with Jesus into the desert.[1]

In this first meeting we shall attempt to experience what 'to walk with Jesus into the desert' entails. During this meeting, we shall place the spotlight on Jesus as he enters the desert prior to beginning his public ministry here on earth. We do this by reading a familiar passage of Scripture and by trying to engage with it with all of our senses. Our aim is to seek to learn from Jesus so that we may become more like him. We prepare ourselves by 'dialling down' – that is, by handing to God some of the pressures that we inevitably bring with us to a gathering like this.

Visual focus

Place on a table or on the floor in the centre of the room: a picture of the desert or a stone or pile of stones that look like pitta bread. (Flat pebbles are ideal.) You could even place a pitta bread beside the stone(s).

Group preparation

- Listen to the hymn 'Forty days and forty nights'[2]
- If you can, echo in your heart some of the sentiments of that hymn that asks God to:
  - enable us to stay with Jesus in his suffering
  - summon up the strength to resist temptation as Jesus did in the desert
  - live so close to Christ during Lent that, when Easter Day arrives, we may rejoice deeply
- Now, be still for a few minutes. Let go of the pressures or plans or excitements you brought to the meeting with you. Be aware of the presence of God in the room where you are meeting. Open yourself to receive all that God wants to give you and show you and teach you in this place.

---

1. Thomas Merton, *Meditation on Liturgy* (Oxford, Mowbrays, 1976), p. 101.
2. You will find this hymn on the cassette *Hymns Ancient and Modern: Hymns for Lent, Holy Week and Easter*, produced by the Portsmouth Cathedral Choir.

Scripture focus

The passage from the Bible that we will focus on in this meeting starts with Jesus' baptism in the River Jordan:

> The moment Jesus came up out of the baptismal waters, the skies opened up and he saw God's Spirit – it looked like a dove – descending and landing on him. And along with the Spirit, a voice: 'This is my Son, chosen and marked by my love, delight of my life.'
>
> Next Jesus was taken into the wild by the Spirit for the Test. The Devil was ready to give it. Jesus prepared for the Test by fasting forty days and forty nights. That left him, of course, in a state of extreme hunger, which the Devil took advantage of in the first test: 'Since you are God's Son, speak the word that will turn these stones into loaves of bread.'
>
> Jesus answered by quoting Deuteronomy: 'It takes more than bread to stay alive. It takes a steady stream of words from God's mouth.'
>
> For the second test the Devil took him to the Holy City. He sat him on top of the Temple and said, 'Since you are God's Son, jump.' The Devil goaded him by quoting Psalm 91: 'He has placed you in the care of angels. They will catch you so that you won't so much as stub your toe on a stone.'
>
> Jesus countered with another citation from Deuteronomy: 'Don't you dare test the Lord your God.'
>
> For the third test, the Devil took him on the peak of a huge mountain. He gestured expansively, pointing out all the earth's kingdoms, how glorious they all were. Then he said, 'They're yours – lock, stock, and barrel. Just go down on your knees and worship me, and they're yours.'
>
> Jesus' refusal was curt: 'Beat it, Satan!' He backed his rebuke with a third quotation from Deuteronomy: 'Worship the Lord your God, and only him. Serve him with absolute single-heartedness.'
>
> The Test was over. The Devil left. And in his place, angels! Angels came and took care of Jesus' needs.'
>
> *Matthew 3:17-4:1-11 (The Message)*

Comment

As I have explained in the Introduction to this book, one of the most powerful ways of walking with Jesus is to engage, not just our minds, but *all of our senses*. That is why, in this section, we look for answers to the following questions:

What did Jesus see and hear, sense and taste – and feel?

As you read this section, try to picture the desert where Jesus spent these forty days:

What did Jesus see?

- The wonder of the sunrise and the sunset that the Psalmist describes so well when he writes:

  The heavens declare the glory of God;
  the skies proclaim the work of his hands . . .
  Psalm 19:1 (NIV)

- the accompanying kaleidoscope of colour
- the star-studded sky that the Psalmist calls 'the starry host' (Psalm 33:6) and that Eugene Peterson calls 'God's handmade jewelry'
- the occasional flower
- the welcome *wadi* from which he could drink pure, clean, life-giving water
- stretches of yellow sand
- vast expanses of crumbling, blistering, peeling limestone,
- scattered shingle
- hills that look like dust heaps
- bare, jagged rocks
- ground shimmering and glowing with heat as intense as a furnace
- ground from which tower contorted strata – where seemingly warped and twisted ridges run in all directions.[1]

What did Jesus feel?

- The searing, sizzling, energy-sapping heat from which, according to the Psalmist,

  Nothing is hidden
  Psalm 19:6 (NIV)

- Exhilaration and awe as he watched the wonder of the sunrise that, again, the Psalmist sums up so poetically:

---

1. For further descriptions and photographs of the Judaean desert see Joyce Huggett, *Formed by the Desert* (Guildford, Eagle, 1997 and 2000).

> The heavens declare the glory of God;
> the skies proclaim the work of his hands . . .
> In the heavens he has pitched a tent for the sun,
> which is like a bridegroom coming
> forth from his pavilion,
> like a champion rejoicing to run his course.
> It rises at one end of the heavens
> and makes its circuit to the other;
> nothing is hidden from its heat.
> *Psalm 19:1, 4b, 5, 6 (NIV)*

- Equal awe as he watched the sun set and as he drank draughts of the deep-down stillness that overwhelms desert dwellers and pilgrims alike

- Lonely

- Hungry

What did Jesus sense?

- The overwhelming, never-failing love of his Father that he had been reminded of when he emerged from the waters of baptism just before the Spirit thrust him into the desert:

  You are my Son, chosen and marked by my love, pride of my life.
  Luke 3:22 (The Message)

What did Jesus hear?

- Ground that sounds hollow to the footsteps

- A deafening silence

- His innermost being asking the question:

  'How am I going to win the world for my Father?'

- Tempting voices whispering:

  Seek popularity – feed the poor by turning stones into bread. They'll love you and follow you.

  Seek power – impress the crowd by jumping. God will keep you safe.

Seek possessions – accumulate all the land you can. You will be famous and people will envy you and flock to you.

Personal exploration

- Close your eyes and try to picture Jesus in the desert. What can you see?
- As you watch, what makes the deepest impression on you?
- Listen to the way Jesus deals with the Tempter. How do you feel about Jesus' strength and singleness of vision and about his life motto:

I have come to do your will, O God.

Hebrews 10:7b (NIV)

Personal sharing

Is there anything you would like to share with the group in the light of that period of personal reflection – something you saw or what it was that made the deepest impression on you? You have an opportunity now to enrich the group with your personal insights.

Group discussion

- Satan tried to persuade Jesus to launch his earthly ministry by seeking power, prestige and popularity and by accumulating possessions. These temptations are subtle and as much in vogue today as they were when Jesus lived on earth. Where do we see leaders today capitulating to these inner compulsions?
- These temptations come to *every* Christian. How can we resist them?

Worship time

Some groups might like to begin this time of worship by lighting a candle that has been placed in a prominent position in the room. As someone has expressed it:

> Lighting a candle is a parable. Burning itself out, a candle gives light to others reminding us that Jesus gave *himself* for others and calls us to give ourselves also.[1]

- Listen to the Taizé chant: 'Stay here and keep watch with me . . .'[2]

---

1. I found these insights on a prayer card in a country church on the Isle of Wight.

2. This chant may be found on many cassettes and CDs including *Taizé Chants,* produced by the St Thomas' Music Group directed by Margaret Rizza, published by Alliance Music.

- Pray the following prayer that is based on Philippians 2:6. One member of the group could read the sentences in bold print while everyone else says the words that appear in italics:

Jesus set aside the privileges of deity
and took on the status of a slave.

Lord, give me the grace to serve others.

Jesus refused to claim privileges.
He lived a selfless life,
and died a selfless death.

Lord, purge me of self-centredness.

The hallmark of Jesus' life
was obedience.
His motto was:
'I have come to do *your* will, O God.'

Lord, may my motto, too,
goad me to live life your way –
the way of willing obedience to your plan for me,
that I may glorify Jesus.
Amen.

Listen to the song 'In the desert'[1] sung by Michael Card or 'To love only you'[2]
Say together:

Great God of the desert,
as we pursue life's path,
alert us to the tempter's ploys,
equip us to resist his subtle suggestions,
and empower us to love,
serve,
and worship
you alone.

---

1. This song has been composed by and is sung by Michael Card on the CD and cassette *The Ancient Faith*.
2. You will find this song on the *Open to God* cassette, published by Eagle.

Week 2

Round the Upper Room

This week, as we move from the desert to the Upper Room, we focus on the way Jesus washed his disciples' dusty, sweaty feet and seek to discover what it means to love as he does.

Visual focus

Place on a table or in the centre of the room, a bowl, a jug of water and a towel. Or enlarge the picture on page 28, laminate it if possible and use that as a visual aid.

Group preparation

- Listen to the Taizé chant: 'O Lord, hear my prayer'.[1]
- Be still for several minutes. Tell God what you hope for from this meeting.
- In the stillness be aware of God's presence in the room with you now.
- When God is present, love is present because love is what God is.
- Be aware that God loves *you* – uniquely and unconditionally.
- So hand to God the pressures, problems and excitements that might prevent you from participating in this meeting.
- Now relax in his attentive presence. Be assured that he cares about *you*.
- Prepare yourself to receive the insights that will come to you through the passage of Scripture that follows.

Scripture focus

A member of the group will now read the following:

Before the festival of the Passover began, Jesus realised that the time had come for him to leave this world and return to the Father. He had loved those who were his own in this world and he loved them to the end. By supper-time, the devil had already put the thought of betraying Jesus into the mind of Judas Iscariot, Simon's son. Jesus, with the full

---

1. You will find this chant on various CDs and cassettes produced by the Taizé community in France. It also features on the CD and cassette *Taizé Chants*, produced by the St Thomas' Music Group directed by Margaret Rizza and produced by Alliance Music.

knowledge that the Father had put everything into his hands and that he had come from God and was going to God, rose from the supper-table, took off his outer clothes, picked up a towel and fastened it around his waist. Then he poured water into the basin and began to wash the disciples' feet and to dry them with the towel around his waist.

So he came to Simon Peter, who said to him, 'Lord, are you going to wash my feet?'

'You do not realise now what I am doing,' replied Jesus, 'but later on you will understand.'

Then Peter said to him, 'You must never wash my feet!'

'Unless you let me wash you, Peter,' replied Jesus, 'you cannot share my lot.'

'Then,' returned Simon Peter, 'please – not just my feet but my hands and my face as well!'

'The man who has bathed,' returned Jesus, 'only needs to wash his feet to be clean all over. And you are clean – though not all of you.'

(For Jesus knew his betrayer and that is why he said 'though not all of you'.)

When Jesus had washed their feet and put on his clothes, he sat down again and spoke to them, 'Do you realise what I have just done to you? You call me "teacher" and "Lord" and you are quite right, for I am your teacher and your Lord. But if I, your teacher and Lord, have washed your feet, you must be ready to wash one another's feet. I have given you this as an example so that you may do as I have done.'
John 13:1-16 JBP[1]

Comment

For many years now, it has become customary in some Churches to remember the institution of The Last Supper by holding a Communion Service in Church on the Thursday evening immediately preceding Good Friday. Last year, on Maundy Thursday evening, I attended one of

---

1. *New Testament in Modern English*, J. B. Phillips (London, Geoffrey Bles, 1960), pp. 221-222.

these services. Before the service began, we had been warned that, before we received the bread and the wine, there would be a 'foot washing' ceremony. *'If you would like to take part, come prepared!'* the notice read. Those of us who wanted to participate made sure that all we had to do at the appropriate moment in the service was to slip off our shoes and sit bare-footed.

The service began with a hymn and the usual prayers followed by the reading from John 13 that you have just read. The person who happens to be my Spiritual Director then got up out of her chair, carefully and reverently wrapped a towel around her waist and walked to the prominent place in the chapel where a jug of water had been placed. Quietly and reverently, she poured the water into a bowl before carefully carrying it to the circle where we were all sitting. There, she started to wash the feet of members of the congregation who had removed their shoes. As I watched, I was deeply moved by the care and tenderness with which she appeared to be both washing and wiping their feet.

As she approached *me*, though, suddenly, I was horrified. 'How can I let my *Spiritual Director* wash *my* feet?' I asked myself. She knows so much about me. I should be washing *her* feet.

She came. Quietly and gently she washed my right foot, then dried it, even separating my toes and wiping between them. As she did so, suddenly I understood why Peter protested when Jesus approached him. Peter, the unworthy one, was being washed by the spotless Lamb of God just as I, the unworthy one, was being given the privilege of being washed by someone who has travelled deeper into God than I have.

Kevin Scully claims that re-enacting the 'foot-washing' in this way 'is a ceremony which is both moving and revolting. Those who have agreed or been selected to take part often wonder if their feet will be good enough. Some even anticipate the event by giving their toes a good scrub before the occasion. It is as though, while taking a role, they would like to distance themselves . . . from this rather unsavoury piece of theatre. These reactions capture the response of the disciples.'[1] I understood and identified with that claim that Thursday evening in Holy Week.

As we noted in the Introduction to this book, Kevin Scully also reminds us that our senses are an invaluable aid to our contemplation of the events

1. Kevin Scully, *Sensing the Passion* (London, SPCK, Triangle, 1997), p. 63.

that led up to the death of Jesus. 'They link us to him. His experiences were complete human experiences. His sight was like our sight. His hearing was like our hearing. His touch was like our touch. His sense of smell was like ours. His taste was like our taste.'[1]

For this reason, once again, we home in on the same questions as last week – starting with 'What did Jesus see?'

What did Jesus see?

By the time Jesus reached the Upper Room, the meal had already been prepared. So, when Jesus arrived, he saw, not only the group of disciples who so eagerly anticipated sharing this feast with him, he also saw the ready-prepared table. In Exodus 12, we are given such a graphic description of the Passover meal that it is not difficult for us to imagine the array of food that confronted Jesus. So, among other delicacies, he would have seen the following:

- A shank bone of sizzling, spit-roasted lamb, that would remind him and the disciples of the lamb that was offered during the first Passover meal

- Bowls of bitter herbs that provided a powerful reminder that the years of slavery had been both embittered and full of hardship

- A colourful selection of other herbs including endive and chicory

- A dish of unleavened bread – that is bread without yeast – reminding him, among other things, of the three patriarchs: Abraham, Isaac and Jacob

- A special paste in which stood sticks of cinnamon. The paste was called *Cheroseth* and consisted of a mixture of nuts, finely chopped apples, dates, pomegranates, cinnamon and wine. This dish was symbolic of the clay and straw the Hebrew slaves were forced to use when they made bricks in Egypt

- A plate of celery or parsley that prompted them to thank God for springtime and the goodness of his earth

- A bowl of salt water that reminded him of the tears the Hebrews shed while they were slaves in Egypt and of the salt waters of the Red Sea through which God's hand had so miraculously brought them.

---

1. Ibid, p. 2.

- Jesus would also have seen the goblets. During the meal, each person was expected to drink four cups of wine that represented for them the blood that the Hebrews sprinkled on their door posts at Passover time. The wine was also symbolic of the four stages through which the Hebrews had been released from slavery.[1]

In other words, even before the foot-washing and the institution by Jesus of 'The Last Supper', the Passover was a very special meal for Jesus and his disciples.

What did Jesus hear during this final meal with his disciples?

- Peter's protest: 'You must never wash my feet!'
- The disciples bickering over which of them was 'the greatest' (See Luke 22:24).

What did Jesus smell?

- The aroma of the barbecued lamb, the herbs, the wine . . .

What did Jesus sense?

- Judas' resolve to betray him as soon as he could escape from this special supper
- Peter's inability to live up to his determination to support Jesus; his impending denial of the Lord he loved
- The stark realisation that none of his disciples would be able to stay with him in the testing time that lay ahead of him as he suffered and died.

Personal exploration

Be still now. Picture the Upper Room where Jesus and the disciples are enjoying this special Passover meal. In your imagination, step into that room. Watch Jesus carefully. Ask yourself: 'What does he touch or hold?'

Then ask yourself, 'Is there anything I would like to say to him?' In the silence of your heart, speak to him.

---

1. In this section I am drawing heavily on the insights of Kevin Scully in *Sensing the Passion*, p. 45.

Personal sharing

If you would like to, enrich the group by telling them some of the things you saw and heard and sensed during that time of personal reflection. Remember to follow each person's sharing with a few seconds of silence before moving on to the next person.

Group discussion

The person who normally washed the feet of guests at a special meal like this was *a slave* – certainly not the honoured guest. Why do you think Jesus assumed this role on this very special occasion?

Might it be helpful for you as a group to have a foot-washing ceremony just before Easter? If not, why not? If so, what do you think it might do for the group? When do you think you should have it?

Worship time

Listen to the chorus: 'The Servant King'[1]

Say the following prayer together slowly and meditatively:

The Saviour of the world
wraps a towel around his waist.
Holding a bowl in both hands,
he moves around the circle of his friends
washing their sweaty, sandy feet,
touching their toughened toenails,
wiping between those toes.

With his hands he speaks to them
with his eyes he loves them
by his tenderness he melts them
with his lips he pleads with them
to love as he loves.

So let us learn how to serve
by our lives to reveal him –

---

1. Graham Kendrick CD, *The Graham Kendrick Easter Collection*, (Kevin Mayhew, 2000).

meeting each other's needs,
recognising that, in serving others,
it is Jesus *we are serving.*

Listen to the song 'Brother, sister let me serve you'[1]

Pause to ask God whether there is anyone you can serve sacrificially and tenderly in the week that lies ahead.

Preparing for next week

Next week, the suggested visual focus is a loaf of bread or some pitta bread. It is just possible that someone in the group loves cooking – in which case they might be willing to *make* some bread. If not, decide who will supply the bread for the visual aid.

Read either Matthew 26:26-28 or Mark 14:22-24 before next week's meeting.

---

1. This song is featured on the CD and cassette *Joy to the World*, produced by Eagle.

Week 3

Through the Last Supper

This week, after we have prepared ourselves to engage afresh with God and his Word, we focus on, reflect on and discuss the moving way in which Jesus instituted the Last Supper. After that, we spend a few minutes in quiet worship.

Visual focus

Place on a table that everyone can see or on a cloth on the floor in the centre of the room a loaf of bread, a bread roll or some pitta bread together with a goblet or special wine glass. You might also like to photocopy and enlarge today's picture and place that where everyone can see it.

Group preparation

- Focus for several seconds on the visual aid in front of you. Let it remind you of the special subject we are focusing on this week: the use Jesus made of bread and wine during The Last Supper.

- This story is more than worthy of our full concentration so be aware of any worries or pressures or excitements that would so preoccupy your mind and heart that you would be unable to focus fully on Jesus in the Upper Room. Hand these potential obstacles to God.

- Now, in the silence, offer yourself to God: your heart as well as your mind, your imagination as well as your brain – and all of your senses. Open yourself to allow God to use each of these as he chooses.

- Pray the prayer the young Samuel once prayed:

  'Speak, Lord, for your servant is listening . . .'

- Listen to the Taizé chant: 'Eat this bread . . .'[1]

Scripture focus

The chant we have just heard takes us back to the place where we were last week – into the Upper Room with Jesus and his disciples.

During the meal, Jesus took and blessed the bread, broke it, and gave it to his disciples:

---

1. You will find this chant on the CD and cassette *Wait for the Lord*, published by Eagle.

'Take, eat.
This is my body.'

Taking the cup and thanking God, he gave it to them:

'Drink this, all of you.
This is my blood,
God's new covenant poured out for many people
for the forgiveness of sins.

I'll not be drinking wine from this cup again until that new day when I'll drink with you in the kingdom of my Father.'
Matthew 26:26-28 (The Message)

During supper, when Jesus uttered these never-to-be-forgotten words:

He saw

- Judas' eyes as, together, they dipped their bread in one of the dishes
- Peter's anger (see Mark 14:29)
- Judas' growing impatience
- Judas leaving the room
- The troubled faces of the eleven disciples when they heard that one of them would betray Jesus
- The bread that he was about to bless and use to symbolise his own body
- The wine that he was also about to bless and use to represent his blood
- The eyes of those who watched him break the bread
- The fingers of those who responded to his request to drink the wine
- The reactions to his claim as he broke the bread and uttered that unforgettable claim:

    'This is my body . . .'

- The response as he added the claim when he blessed the wine:

    'This is my blood . . .'

- The disciples' reaction as he departed from the normal Passover liturgy and introduced his own clauses

He heard

- The camaraderie and the animated conversation as his disciples tucked into the feast
- The sound of wine being poured into goblets
- The clatter of bowls and dishes and plates
- The involuntary gasp that some disciples uttered when he broke the news that one of them would betray him
- The question many of them asked: *'Is it I?'*
- John's whispered question: *'Who is it?'*
- The snap as he broke the bread
- The sound of the bread being sucked, chewed, then swallowed
- The sound of the wine being sipped

He smelt

- The sweaty bodies of the friends he loved so much
- The aroma of:
  - the barbecued lamb
  - the herbs and spices
  - the freshly baked bread

He felt

- Desolate (John 13:21)
- The affection John the Beloved was expressing so openly

He tasted – that is, he had a foretaste of

- Betrayal
- Denial
- Death by crucifixion
- Burial

Personal reflection

Be still now. Close your eyes. Picture the Upper Room again and use your God-given gift of the imagination. Listen to the disciples. Then focus on

Jesus. Look at his face as he rises from the table. See him take a piece of bread from the dish. Watch how he breaks it. Look carefully as he holds high the goblet of wine and blesses it. Now focus on your God-given gift of hearing. Listen to Jesus say of the bread:

'This is my body broken for you . . .'

Hear him say to you:

'Take and eat . . .'

Hear Jesus continue as he offers you the goblet of wine:

'This is my blood . . .'

'Drink . . .'

Notice the tone of his voice. What does it sound like? Does it make you want to do as he asks: to receive and eat the bread, to drink the wine? If so, what is it about his voice that woos you in this way?

Turn your reactions and responses and reflections over and over in your heart and mind for a few minutes. Is there anything you would like to say to Jesus by way of response?

Personal sharing

This week, instead of inviting group members to share with everyone, divide the group into pairs. Allow six minutes for this time of sharing. One person will share with the person sitting next to them what they saw or heard or what made the biggest impact on them during that time of reflection. After three minutes, the group leader will need to remind the group that it is time to allow the second person to speak. Alternatively, you could set a timer to ring after three minutes. Its ring would signify that it is time for the second person in the twosome to share what she or he has heard and seen and what made the biggest impact on *them*.

Group discussion

As you move into discussion, remember that your aim is to *learn* from one another and be enriched by each other not to compete with each other, put one another down or criticise another's contribution.

On that unforgettable night, the disciples thought they were going to enjoy a traditional Passover meal with Jesus. Instead, they found themselves attending the first Last Supper (or, as some Christians call it, the first service of Communion or Holy Communion; the first Eucharist[1] or Breaking of Bread). What are some of the thoughts that might have passed through their minds when they remembered Jesus' insistence that they should *'do this in remembrance of me'*?

How do *you* feel about that request that Jesus made?

What dissuades today's Christians from doing as Jesus asked?

Worship time

Listen to the song 'Take this bread' by Paul Gurr,[2] or listen again to the song 'Eat this bread'.

Now take the bread that you have used as a visual aid during your meeting and pass it around the group. Recalling the words of Jesus to: *'Take . . . eat . . .'*, when the loaf or roll or pitta bread reaches you, picture Jesus standing in front of you reminding you of that invitation. Break off a piece of bread and eat it before you pass the loaf to the person sitting next to you. Then, in the stillness, pray your own prayer of thanks.

When everyone has received the bread, say the following prayer together:

> *Washer of feet – cleanse me*
> *Breaker of bread – feed me*
> *Giver of wine –*
> *fill me with your life-blood*
> *and give me an ever-grateful heart.*

Listen to the song: 'Broken for me, broken for you'.[3]

---

1. The word Eucharist is a rather lovely way of describing this meal. It stems from the Greek word that simply means *thank you*.

2. This song may be found on the CD and cassette *Come As You Are*, published by Spectrum Productions, Australia.

3. You will find this song on the CD and cassette *Wait for the Lord*, produced by The Jane Lilley Singers, published by Eagle.

Week 4

To the Garden of Gethsemane

This week, we walk from the Upper Room, across the Kidron Valley to the Garden of Gethsemane. There, we catch a glimpse of what it cost Jesus to give up his life to rescue us.

Visual focus

Find a picture of The Garden of Gethsemane and place it where everyone can see it. Or enlarge and laminate the picture that appears on page 47 of this book and place that somewhere central.

Group preparation

This week's story is so sorrowful and powerful that we need to give it our full attention. So be still for a few minutes. In the stillness, become aware of any anxieties or excitements, any distractions or desires that would prevent you from focusing fully on Jesus. Hand these potential obstacles to God. Entrust them to his care. Become aware of his presence with you as you ask for the grace to do what Jesus asked his disciples to do: to stay with him in his suffering.

Scripture focus

Then Jesus went with them to a garden called Gethsemane and told his disciples, 'Stay here while I go over there and pray.' Taking along Peter and the two sons of Zebedee, he plunged into an agonizing sorrow. Then he said, 'This sorrow is crushing my life out. Stay here and keep vigil with me.'

Going a little ahead, he fell on his face, praying, 'My Father, if there is any way, get me out of this. But please, not what I want. You, what do *you* want?'

When he came back to his disciples, he found them sound asleep. He said to Peter, 'Can't you stick it out with me a single hour? Stay alert; be in prayer so you don't wander into temptation without even knowing you're in danger. There is a part of you that is eager, ready for anything in God. But there's another part that's as lazy as an old dog sleeping by the fire.'

He then left them a second time. Again he prayed, 'My Father, if there is no other way than this, drinking this cup to the dregs, I'm ready. Do it your way.'

When he came back . . . he found them sound asleep. They simply couldn't keep their eyes open. This time he let them sleep on, and went back a third time to pray, going over the same ground one last time.

When he came back the next time, he said, 'Are you going to sleep on and make a night of it? My time is up, the Son of Man is about to be handed over to the hands of sinners. Get up! Let's get going! My betrayer is here.'

Matthew 26:36-46 (The Message)

Comment

When Jesus walked this earth, many wealthy people had private gardens on the Mount of Olives. It would appear that one of them had given Jesus permission to use his garden – the garden of Gethsemane – and that Jesus went there often to be alone with his Father. When the Last Supper was over, Jesus and all his disciples except Judas, made their way across the Kidron valley to this garden.

On this unforgettable night, Jesus felt keenly the need of the support of the three special friends who seem to have been closest to him: Peter, James and John. Like all the other disciples, though, these men were weary after a busy day of preparing for and celebrating the Passover. While Jesus descended into a dark pit of despair, like all the other disciples, these three trusted, privileged friends *slept,* leaving Jesus to fight his frightening battle alone.

As William Barclay recalls the moment:

Jesus was only 33, and no one wants to die at 33. He knew what crucifixion was like; He had seen it. He was in an *agony*; the Greek word is used of someone who is fighting a battle with sheer fear. There is no scene like this in all history. This was the very hinge and turning point in Jesus' life. He could have turned back even yet. He could have refused the Cross. The salvation of the whole world hung in the balance as the Son of God literally sweated it out in Gethsemane; and he won . . . he went into Gethsemane in agony, he came out with the victory won, and with peace in his soul – because he had talked with God.[1]

---

1. William Barclay, *The Daily Study Bible: The Gospel of Luke* (Edinburgh, The Saint Andrew Press, 1958), pp. 283-284.

What did Jesus see in Gethsemane?

- The olive grove that had been his refuge so often
- The silver light of the moon filtering through the branches of the ancient olive trees
- A myriad of stars peering down at him from the darkness of the canopy of heaven
- His sleeping disciples

What did Jesus feel?

- The cool evening breeze
- Fear
- Dread
- Grief
- Loneliness
- Sorrow (Matthew 26:37)
- Desperation (v. 40)
- Anguish (v. 39)
- A deep desire and determination to do the Father's will (Mark 14:35)
- Forsaken by the disciples

What did Jesus hear?

- His own voice protesting, pleading, screaming
- The snores of his sleeping disciples
- The rustling of the leaves of the trees
- His own heartbeat
- His own sighs and groans
- The constant chorus of the cicadas
- The sound of the tramp, tramp, tramp of his captors' footsteps drawing ever closer

What did Jesus sense?

- Impending doom
- Judas' imminent arrival and betrayal
- The nearness of death
- The inattentiveness of the disciples – even of Peter and John

What did Jesus smell?

- The fragrance of the scents of springtime: olive blossom, almond blossom, the abundance of wild flowers that spring up in this part of the world at this time of year
- The tinge of the smell of herbs and barbecued lamb on his hands and his clothes
- The freshness of the great outdoors

Personal reflection

Close your eyes and, in your imagination, walk with Jesus into the Garden of Gethsemane. Do as he asks: 'Keep watch . . .' with him. Sense his anguish and dread and pain. Watch him surrender to his Father with that unforgettable resolve: *'Not as I will, but as you will.'* How do you feel about this man who loves you so much that he is saying 'yes' to death – *for you*?

Is there anything you would like to say to him? If so, write it in the form of a prayer.

Personal sharing

Turn to the person sitting next to you. Share with that person just one thing that you saw or heard or felt during that period of reflection. Then, if you wrote a prayer, and if you would like to, read aloud the prayer that you wrote.

Group discussion

The Garden of Gethsemane is famous because it became the place where Jesus cried: *'I can't but I will.'* Can you think of occasions when you have similarly surrendered to the will of God in difficult circumstances? Or can you think of others known to you who have whispered *'Your will be done . . .'* to God? Tell the story of such occasions now. Keep the story-telling brief so that there is time to discuss what members of the group feel they can learn from such Christ-like examples of surrender to the will of God.

Worship time

- Listen to the request Jesus made of his disciples in the Garden of Gethsemane by playing the Taizé chant: 'Stay here and keep watch with me'[1]

- Picture Jesus in the garden – weeping, crying, protesting, agonising – then submitting. Then say the following sentence together – slowly, gratefully:

> He did it for me . . .
> He did it for *me* . . .
> He did it *for me* . . .

- Jesus surrendered his life and his death into the Father's hands. Has God been asking you to surrender to him in any way in recent days, weeks, months, years? If so, would it be possible for you to follow the example of Jesus and to surrender by making a mini-surrender to him before Easter?

- Listen to the way Jesus made his exit from the Garden of Gethsemane:

---

1. You will find this chant on the CD and cassette *Taizé Chants*, directed by Margaret Rizza, sung by the St Thomas' Group, and on the CD and cassette *Stay With Me*, sung by The Jane Lilley Singers, published by Eagle Publishing.

Judas who betrayed him knew the [garden], for Jesus often met his disciples there. So Judas fetched the guard and the officers which the chief priest and Pharisees had provided for him, and came to the place with torches and lanterns and weapons. Jesus, fully realising all that was going to happen to him, went forward and said to them, 'Who are you looking for?'

'Jesus of Nazareth,' they answered.

'I am the man,' said Jesus . . .

When he said to them, 'I am the man', they retreated and fell to the ground. So Jesus asked them again, 'Who are you looking for?'

And again they said, 'Jesus of Nazareth.'

'I have told you that I am the man,' replied Jesus. 'If I am the man you are looking for, let these others go.' (Thus fulfilling his previous words, 'I have not lost one of those whom you gave me.')
John 18:1ff (J. B. Phillips)

Jesus, the one who healed so many people, taught so many people, the one who initiated the Last Supper, no longer controls anything or anyone. From now, until his death, he becomes the one who is acted upon rather than the one who acts. The result? His divinity shines through his humanity as it did on the Mount of Transfiguration. His captors are so overwhelmed by him that they fall to the ground. Although he is weak, he has great strength and his glory can be glimpsed. Although he is held captive, he continues to love. As the thirteenth-century mystic, Julian of Norwich, put it:

Love was his meaning

Listen to the chorus: 'Such love'[1]

---

1. This chorus has been beautifully recorded by The Jane Lilley Singers on *Stay With Me* (CD and cassette), published by Eagle.

Say this prayer together:

Holy, holy, holy,
vulnerable God,
heaven and earth are full of your glory;
hosanna in the highest.
blessed is the one
who goes to the gallows in the name of God;
hosanna in the highest.[1]

Preparing for next week

Before next week's meeting, read Matthew 26:47-67 and ask someone to photocopy the picture on page 56 and to enlarge and laminate it so that it can be placed in a central place as a visual aid.

---

1. An adaptation of part of a prayer written for the Greenham vigil on Maundy Thursday, 1987. The original prayer is quoted in Janet Morley, *All Desires Known* (London, SPCK, 1992), p. 50.

Week 5

To the High Priest's Palace

Last week we left Jesus in the hands of Judas, his betrayer, and the cohort of soldiers who had seized him in the garden of Gethsemane. This week, together with Peter, we follow Jesus out of the garden and into the courtyard of the palace of Caiaphas, the High Priest. First, we start by praying together the words of a well-loved hymn:

> O teach me what it meaneth,
> that cross uplifted high,
> with Thee, the Man of Sorrows,
> condemned to bleed and die;
> O teach me what it meaneth,
> that sacred crimson tide,
> the blood and water flowing
> from Thine own wounded side.
>
> O teach me what it meaneth,
> for I am full of sin;
> and grace alone can reach me,
> and love alone can win.
> Teach me that if none other
> had sinned, but I alone,
> yet still Thy blood, Lord Jesus,
> thine only, must atone.
>
> O teach me what it meaneth,
> thy love beyond compare,
> the love that reacheth deeper
> than depths of self-despair;
> yes, teach me, till there gloweth
> in this cold heart of mine,
> some feeble, pale reflection
> of that pure love of Thine.

Lucy Ann Bennett, 1850-1927

Group preparation

With the words of that hymn ringing in your ears, open yourself to God in the same way as a water lily opens to the warmth of the sunshine. Ask God to touch your eyes and ears, your mind and your imagination, your heart and your will so that, as a result of this meeting, you will be able to see him more clearly, love him more fervently and become more like him each day as Easter approaches and beyond.

Scripture focus

Arresting Jesus, they marched him off and took him into the house of the Chief Priest. Peter followed, but at a safe distance. In the middle of the courtyard some people had started a fire and were sitting around it, trying to keep warm. One of the serving maids sitting at the fire noticed him, then took a second look and said, 'This man was with him!'

He denied it, 'Woman, I don't even know him.'

A short time later, someone else noticed him and said, 'You're one of them.'

But Peter denied it: 'Man, I am not.'

About an hour later, someone else spoke up, really adamant: 'He's got to have been with him! He's got "Galilean" written all over him.'

Peter said, 'Man, I don't know what you're talking about.' At that very moment, the last word hardly off his lips, a rooster crowed. Just then, the Master turned and looked at Peter. Peter remembered what the Master had said to him: 'Before the rooster crows, you will deny me three times.' He went out and cried and cried and cried.

Luke 22:54-62 (The Message)

Comment

In his book, *The Song of the Bird*, Anthony de Mello recalls an occasion when, like Peter, he felt the eyes of Jesus talking to him:

In the gospel according to Luke we read the following:

But Peter said, 'Man, I do not know what you are talking about.' At that moment while he was still speaking a cock crowed, and the Lord turned and looked straight at Peter . . . and Peter went outside and wept.

I had a fairly good relationship with the Lord. I would ask him for things, converse with him, praise him, thank him.

But always I had this uncomfortable feeling that he wanted me to look into his eyes. And I would not. I would talk, but look away when I sensed that he was looking at me.

I always looked away. And I knew why. I was afraid. I thought I should find an accusation there of some unrepented sin. I thought I should find a demand there, there would be something he wanted from me.

One day I finally summoned up courage and looked! There was no accusation. There was no demand. The eyes just said, 'I love you.' I looked long into those eyes. I looked searchingly. Still the only message was, 'I love you.'

And I walked out, and like Peter, I wept.[1]

Personal reflection

Picture Peter in that courtyard. Hear him insist that he did not know Jesus. Now picture Jesus gazing at the disciple he loved denying the Master he had vowed he would follow to his death. What do you sense Jesus is trying to communicate to Peter through that gaze? Or, do what Anthony de Mello did – look at Jesus yourself. Be aware that Jesus is gazing on *you*. What do you read in his eyes and his face?

Personal sharing

Form groups of no more than three people. Give each person an opportunity to share a little of what they saw or heard or sensed during that period of reflection. (The reasons why I am suggesting that, this week, you divide into small groups is that some people feel more comfortable sharing in this way rather than a large group.)

Group discussion

Bearing in mind the emphasis we are placing in this booklet on the use of the senses as well as the mind, picture the following sequence of events. The Romans who came forward and arrested Jesus would have been taught the customary way such arrests were conducted.

1. Anthony de Mello, *The Song of the Bird* (Doubleday, 1984).

- Jesus would have been seized by the right wrist.

- His arm would then have been twisted behind him until his knuckles touched the space between his shoulder blades.

- At the same time, his heel would have been forced down onto his right instep and jammed there.

- The other arm would have then been grabbed and thrust behind his back.

- A rope would then have been tied between his hands.

- At the same time, a noose would have been hung around his neck.

As he suffered the indignity, humiliation and shocking pain of this sequence of events, Jesus must have looked a forlorn, even a frightening figure. Having had no sleep or rest and having endured such grief and inner turmoil, the colour would have drained from his face, his eyes would have become bloodshot and blotches of blood may well have dried on his cheeks and clung to his beard. His bare feet must have been filthy and possibly bleeding from the march and his clothing would have been soiled, possibly torn, since he had been kicked, prodded and pushed much of the way.[1]

Respond to the following questions bearing in mind the passage from Matthew that you read at home during the week:

- What did Jesus see as he was led out of the garden and made the journey to the city and to the High Priest's Palace?

- What did he see *in* that palace?

- What might Jesus have heard on the journey?

- What did he hear in the palace?

- How might he have been feeling on this journey?

- How might he have felt while he was being 'tried'?

- What do you think he sensed as his captors led him away?

- What did he sense while the 'court case' was taking place?

---

1. I am leaning here on the insights powerfully portrayed in Jim Bishop, *The Day Christ Died* (London, Collins, Fontana Books, 1967), pp. 213, 222.

Worship time

Listen to or sing the hymn: 'My song is love unknown'.[1]

The following prayer was written in the eleventh century. Join with Christians down the ages and across the world who have echoed these words by saying together:

It is the cup that you drank, Lord Jesus,
  more than anything else
  that makes you love-worthy;
  it is the work of our redemption that supremely claims
  our love.

He put up with people who tried to catch him in his talk,
  carped at his actions,
  mocked his suffering
  and even upbraided him in death.

This love of his is tender,
  wise,
  strong.
Tender in that he took on him our flesh;
  careful and wise in that he guarded against sin;
  and strong in that he suffered death.
I trust myself entirely to him who willed to save me,
  knew the way to do it,
  and had the power to carry out the work.
He has sought me
  and called me by his grace.[2]

---

1. You will find this hymn on a cassette, *Hymns Ancient and Modern: Hymns for Lent, Holy Week and Easter,* produced by the Portsmouth Cathedral Choir.
2. Bernard of Clairvaux (1090-1153) *Selections from the Writings of Bernard Clairvaux,* edited by Douglas V. Steere (London, A. R. Mowbray & Co., 1952).

Listen to the chorus 'O let the Son of God enfold you'[1] then bless each other as you say together the following:

May the Crucified One
give us the grace
to drink in his love
and receive his blessing
this day
this Easter
and into eternity.
Amen.

---

1. This chorus may be found on the *Stay With Me* CD and cassette, performed by The Jane Lilley Singers, published by Eagle.

Week 6

To Golgotha

This week, as we walk with Jesus to Golgotha and see him hanging on the cross, we remind ourselves of his generosity to the dying thief.

Visual focus

Either enlarge and laminate the picture that appears on page 65 or make a cross out of two pieces of wood and lay it on the floor or on a table in the centre of the room.

Group preparation

- Play the Taizé chant: 'O Lord hear my prayer'
- Ask yourself the question: 'What *is* my prayer as we come together to focus on the way Jesus suffered as he carried his cross to Calvary?'
- Write down your prayer before the meeting goes any further

Scripture focus

The soldiers led Jesus away, and as they were going, they met a man from Cyrene named Simon who was coming into the city from the country. They seized him, put the cross on him, and made him carry it behind Jesus.

A large crowd of people followed him; among them were some women who were weeping and wailing for him. Jesus turned to them and said, 'Women of Jerusalem! Don't cry for me, but for yourselves and your children. For the days are coming when people will say, "How lucky are the women who never had children, who never bore babies, who never nursed them!" That will be the time when people will say to the mountains, "Fall on us!" and to the hills, "Hide us!" For if such things as these are done when the wood is green, what will happen when it is dry?'

Two other men, both of them criminals, were also led out to be put to death with Jesus. When they came to the place called 'The Skull,' they crucified Jesus there, and the two criminals, one on his right and the other on his left. Jesus said, 'Forgive them, Father! They don't know what they are doing.'

They divided his clothes among them by throwing dice. The people stood there watching while the Jewish leaders jeered at him:

'He saved others; let him save himself if he is the Messiah whom God has chosen!'

The soldiers also mocked him: they came up to him and offered him cheap wine, and said, 'Save yourself if you are the king of the Jews!'

Above him were written these words: 'This is the King of the Jews!'

One of the criminals hanging there hurled insults at him: 'Aren't you the Messiah? Save yourself and us!'

The other one, however, rebuked him, saying 'Don't you fear God? You received the same sentence he did. Ours, however, is only right, because we are getting what we deserve for what we did; but he has done no wrong.' And he said to Jesus, 'Remember me, Jesus, when you come as King!'

Jesus said to him, 'I promise you that today you will be in Paradise with me.'

It was about twelve o' clock when the sun stopped shining and darkness covered the whole country until three o'clock; and the curtain hanging in the Temple was torn in two. Jesus cried out in a loud voice, 'Father! In your hands I place my spirit!' He said this and died.

Luke 23:26-46 (TEV)

Comment

Commenting on the passage we have just read, William Barclay writes:

The word paradise is a Persian word meaning a *walled garden*. When a Persian king wished to do one of his subjects a very special honour he made him a companion of the garden, and he was chosen to walk in the garden with the king. It was more than immortality that Jesus promised the penitent thief. He promised him the honoured place of the garden in the courts of heaven.

Surely this story tells us above all things that it is never too late to turn to Christ. There are other things of which we must say, 'The time for that is past. I am grown too old for that now.' But we can never say that of turning to Jesus Christ. So long as a [person's] heart beats, the invitation of Christ still stands. As the poet wrote of the man who was killed as he was thrown from his galloping horse,

> 'Between the stirrup and the ground,
> Mercy I asked, mercy I found.'

For us it is literally true that while there is life there is hope.[1]

Personal reflection

In the Introduction to this book, we reminded ourselves that, during Lent, the early Christians learned to ask themselves several questions. One was: *'Do I turn to Christ?'* Another was, *'Do I repent of my sins?'*

Gaze now at the picture of Jesus hanging on the Cross and ask *yourself* these two questions. If you feel you can, make the response that those early Christians made:

The first question was:

Do you turn to Christ?

The response was:

I turn to Christ.

Another question was:

Do you repent of your sins?

The vow stated:

I repent of my sins.

Now, in your imagination, step into the picture of Jesus hanging from the cross. Place yourself alongside the person at the foot of the cross.

Tune in, especially, to the short conversation Jesus had with the penitent thief. What feelings does that conversation stir up in you? Do you have a recurring failure that *you* would like to expose to Jesus – the one who so readily forgave the dying thief? If so, if you feel you can, in the quietness of these few moments of reflection, tell God about it.

---

1. William Barclay, *The Gospel of Luke* (Edinburgh, The St Andrew Press, 1958), p. 300.

Personal sharing

Since our time of reflection this week has been deeply personal, it would probably be inappropriate to invite people to share personally. Move, instead, straight into the group discussion letting your time of reflection determine how you respond to the following questions.

Group discussion

- Simone Weil once wrote:

  'Of all beings other than Christ of whom the Gospel tells us, the just thief is by far the one I most envy.'

  Why do you think she wrote that?

- Why do you think the penitent thief asked Jesus to remember him when Jesus came into his Kingdom? What was he really requesting? Do you think he received what he wanted?

Worship time

- Listen to the Taizé chant that echoes the words of the penitent thief:

  Jesus, remember me when you come into your Kingdom[1]

- Write or draw on a piece of paper a word or a symbol that sums up the failure that you would like to leave at the foot of Christ's cross.

- When everyone is ready, one by one, place your piece of paper as near the cross as possible.

  (As group members do this, play the same Taizé chant again)

- When everyone has placed her or his piece of paper near or on or under the cross, say the following verse from the Bible together:

  If we claim that we're free of sin,
  we're only fooling ourselves.
  A claim like that is errant nonsense.
  On the other hand,
  if we admit our sins –
  make a clean breast of them –

---

1. You can find this chant on the CD and cassette *Taizé Chants*, directed by Margaret Rizza, published by Alliance Music Partners.

he won't let us down;
he'll be true to himself.
He'll forgive our sins
and purge us of all wrongdoing.
1 John 1:9 *(The Message)*

• Now say together this amazing claim:

Nails could not have held
the God-man to the Cross
had not love
held him there.
St Catherine of Siena

• Listen to or sing the hymn 'When I survey the wondrous cross'[1]

When I survey the wondrous cross
on which the Prince of glory died,
my richest gain I count but loss,
and pour contempt on all my pride.

See, from his head, his hands, his feet,
sorrow and love flow mingled down;
did e'er such love and sorrow meet
or thorns compose so rich a crown.
(Isaac Watts, 1674-1748)

---

1. You will find this hymn on the cassette *Hymns Ancient and Modern: Hymns for Lent, Holy Week and Easter,* sung by Portsmouth Cathedral Choir.

Week 7

To the Tomb

This week, we fix our gaze on the most painful day in Jesus' life – the day on which he was crucified. A sacrifice such as the one Jesus made for us demands a response. We seek to make that response in our worship time at the end of this meeting.

Visual focus

Place a large cross or a crucifix or a picture of Jesus hanging from the cross in the middle of the room where everyone can see it.

Group preparation

Listen to or sing the hymn: 'When I survey the wondrous cross'.

Now be still for a few minutes. Be aware that God is in the room with you. Hand to him any thoughts or memories or pressures that would prevent you from focusing fully on the greatest sacrifice that has ever been made. Then, gaze at the picture of Jesus hanging from the cross and remind yourself of an important truth:

He hung there for me

Scripture focus

After they had finished nailing him to the cross and were waiting for him to die, [the soldiers] whiled away the time by throwing dice for his clothes. Above his head they had posted the criminal charge against him: THIS IS JESUS, THE KING OF THE JEWS. Along with him, they also crucified two criminals, one to his right, the other to his left. People passing along the road jeered, shaking their heads in mock lament: 'You bragged that you could tear down the Temple and then rebuild it in three days – so show us your stuff! Save yourself! If you're really God's Son, come down from that cross!'

The high priests, along with the religion scholars and leaders, were right there mixing it up with the rest of them, having a great time poking fun at him: 'He saved others – he can't save himself! King of Israel, is he? Then let him get down from that cross. We'll *all* become believers then! He was so sure of God – well, let him rescue his "Son" now – if he wants him! He did claim to be God's Son, didn't he?' . . .

From noon to three, the whole earth was dark. Around mid-afternoon

Jesus groaned out of the depths, crying loudly, *'Eli, Eli, lama sabachthani?'* which means 'My God, my God, why have you abandoned me?'

Some bystanders who heard him said, 'He's calling for Elijah.' One of them ran and got a sponge soaked in sour wine and lifted it on a stick so he could drink. The others joked, 'Don't be in such a hurry. Let's see if Elijah comes and saves him.'

But Jesus, again crying out loudly, breathed his last.
Matthew 27:33-50 (The Message)

Comment

When someone you love dies, if you have been present in their suffering, when they died and at the burial, you find a strange consolation in remembering the loved-one's final words, how they looked, what they did and so on. Perhaps that is one reason why Christians all over the world seek stillness on Good Friday – particularly between the hours of 12 noon and 3pm: the time when Jesus suffered on the cross, uttered his final words and, breathing his last breath, committed himself to his Father.

Personal reflection

Close your eyes for a few minutes – or gaze at the cross or crucifix or picture of Jesus that serves as your visual focus during this meeting. Ask yourself the following questions:

As Jesus hung on the cross –

- What did he see?
- What did he hear?
- How did he feel?
- What did he smell?
- What did he sense?
- What did he say?

Now repeat to yourself those words that we emphasised earlier:

He hung there for me

Ask yourself, 'How do I feel about a God who cares so much about me that he suffers in this way for my sake?'

Personal sharing

Turn to the person next to you and share a few of the insights that came to you as you engaged in that period of reflection

Group discussion

While I was writing this book, my 3-year-old granddaughter came to stay with me. One evening, while I was reading her bedtime stories, she asked for a story about Jesus. We took her favourite 'Jesus book' from the shelf. Opening it, she found a picture of the birth of Jesus and said: 'I like baby Jesus.' Turning the pages and finding several pictures of the adult Saviour, she then announced: 'I don't like the man.' So I read her the story of Jesus' birth. When I had finished, she thumbed through the book again and came across a picture of the Crucifixion. 'Why did they put Jesus on the cross?' she asked. Then, pointing first to one dying thief and then the other she added: 'That man was naughty – and that man was naughty.' Finally, pointing at Jesus, she persisted: 'but Jesus was good. Why did they put him on the cross?'

What would you have said in answer to her question?

Worship time

Listen to the song 'Broken for me'.[1]

Say the following prayers together:

> *Today he who hung the earth upon the waters*
> *is hung upon the cross.*
> *He who is King of the angels is arrayed in a crown of thorns.*
> *He who wraps the heaven in clouds*
> *is wrapped in the purple of mockery.*
> *He who in Jordan set Adam free receives blows upon his face.*
> *The Bridegroom of the Church is transfixed with nails.*
> *The Son of the Virgin is pierced with a spear.*
> *We worship you, Lord Jesus Christ.*
> *Draw us to yourself with bands of love.*
> *Show us the glory of your resurrection.*[2]

---

1. You will find this on the CD and cassette *Wait for the Lord*, produced by The Jane Lilley Singers, published by Eagle.
2. *The Lenten Triodion*, p. 587.

O Lord,
Holy Father,
show me what kind of man it is
who is hanging for our sakes
on the cross,
whose suffering causes the rocks themselves
to crack and crumble with compassion,
whose death brings the dead back to life.
Let my heart crack and crumble
at the sight of him.
Let my soul break apart with compassion
for his suffering.
Let it be shattered with grief at my sins
for which he dies.
And finally let it be softened
with devoted love
for him.
Amen.[1]

Now read how the first Good Friday ended:

When the captain [of the soldiers] saw what happened, he honoured God:

'This man was innocent! A good man, and innocent!'

All who had come around as spectators to watch the show, when they saw what actually happened, were overcome with grief and headed home. Those who knew Jesus well, along with the women who had followed him from Galilee, stood at a respectful distance and kept vigil.

There was a man by the name of Joseph, a member of the Jewish High Council, a man of good heart and good character. He had not gone along with the plans and actions of the council. His hometown was the Jewish village of Arimathea. He lived in alert expectation of the kingdom of God. He went to Pilate and asked for the body of Jesus. Taking him down, he wrapped him in a linen shroud and placed him in a tomb chiseled into the rock, a tomb never yet used. It was the day before Sabbath, the Sabbath just about to begin.

---

1. A prayer from the thirteenth-century Franciscan, Bonaventure.

The women who had been companions of Jesus from Galilee followed along. They saw the tomb where Jesus' body was placed. Then they went back to prepare burial spices and perfumes. They rested quietly on the Sabbath, as commanded.

Luke 23:44-56 (The Message)

Preparing for next week

If possible, bring some spring flowers with you to next week's meeting. You will also need to bring a stone that you can hold in the palm of your hand.

Week 8

On the first Easter Evening

Visual focus

Find a picture of the Risen Christ and place it in a prominent position in the room where you are meeting. Alternatively, decorate the room in which you are meeting with spring flowers placing some, perhaps, at the base of an *empty* cross. Let the shapes and colours and freshness of the flowers symbolise and express the glory of the day of Resurrection.

Group preparation

Listen to 'Mary's Song' on the CD or cassette of Adrian Snell's musical *The Passion*.

On the first Easter Day, Jesus met many of his disciples – either individually or as a group. Today he longs to meet us. We become most conscious of his presence when we are still. So take a few minutes to tune in to the presence of the Risen One – here in the place where you are meeting. Ask for the grace to see him and hear him, to sense him and to feel his love *for you*.

Scripture Focus

Later on that [first day of the week], the disciples had gathered together, but, fearful of the Jews, had locked all the doors in the house. Jesus entered, stood among them, and said, 'Peace to you.' Then he showed them his hands and his side.

The disciples, seeing the Master with their own eyes, were exuberant. Jesus repeated his greeting. 'Peace to you. Just as the Father sent me, I send you.'

Then he took a deep breath and breathed into them.

'Receive the Holy Spirit,' he said. 'If you forgive someone's sins, they're gone for good. If you don't forgive sins, what are you going to do with them?'

John 20:19-23 (The Message)

Comment

One of the most amazing cries Jesus uttered from the cross as he looked down on his murderers, those who had schemed and dreamed of having him flogged, publicly shamed and nailed to a cruel cross, those in the crowd who mocked and scorned him, the friends who had deserted him in his hour of deepest need was:

'Father, forgive them, they don't know what they're doing.'

By seeking out his special friends on the first Easter Day, Jesus was incarnating, that is, fleshing out the art of forgiveness. How did Peter feel when Jesus drew alongside him somewhere in Jerusalem on Resurrection morning? (Luke 24:34). Embarrassed? Ashamed? Fearful? Possibly. After all, three times he had denied that he even knew the Lord he had promised to support to the bitter end. But while they were talking, Jesus must have reassured this disciple who had denied him so fervently, that he harboured no bitterness or resentment or hatred against his all-too-weak disciple. Similarly, by joining his special friends that first Easter evening, Jesus was persuading them that he came to bring peace not to mete out punishment.

People who are working through grief after the death of a loved one often instinctively seek someone to blame: a nurse, a doctor, a relative, themselves. Were the disciples blaming themselves for deserting Jesus as they mulled over the events that culminated in his death? Were they pointing the finger at one another that evening as they sat locked in with their fear and dread? Possibly. If this is what they were doing, it is little wonder that the unexpected arrival of the Risen Lord Jesus filled them with joyful exuberance and it is little wonder that he reminded them of the need to forgive.

The Greek word *'to forgive'* is *aphesis* which means *'to drop'*. As Jesus thrilled his friends with this first, unexpected group encounter with himself, he reminded them of the need to drop any bitterness or blame, resentment or shame they were harbouring. He reminded them, too, to resist finger-pointing, resentment or determination to punish and to open their hearts to receive and give love and peace.

Personal reflection

Leave plenty of time for this period of reflection. In your imagination, step into the room with the disciples. Sit with them. Watch their reaction as Jesus slips into the room so unexpectedly and miraculously. Now fix your gaze on Jesus. Look at him carefully. What do you see? What do you hear him say? How do you sense he feels? How do *you* feel:

- as, at his invitation, you gaze at his nail-pierced hands

- as you see the gash in his side

- as you feel him breathe his own life into you

- as you hear him reminding *you* to forgive

- Is there anything you would like to say to Jesus, the Risen One?

- Is there anything you would like to do?

- In the quietness of your heart, respond in whatever way seems appropriate to you.

Personal sharing

Divide the group into small clusters of not more than three people per cluster. Share with the others in your small group one of the things that you saw or heard or felt or smelt or experienced as you stepped into the room to be with the disciples and with Jesus.

Worship time

- As we have seen in the Gospel reading, when Jesus entered the room where the disciples were hiding on the first Easter Evening, he greeted them in the traditional way with the word, *'Shalom!'* which means peace. Listen to the words of Jesus that have been set to music by Adrian Snell in his musical *The Passion*.

- As we saw in the Introduction to this book, the early converts to Christianity spent the whole of Lent preparing to be admitted as full Church members. On Easter Day, they made their baptismal vows, were baptised and admitted as full Church members. During that memorable service, they prayed the Lord's Prayer for the first time. Read the words of that prayer now. Read them as though you had never seen them before. Then pray them aloud all together:

Our Father in heaven,
hallowed be your name,
your kingdom come,
your will be done,
on earth as in heaven.
Give us today our daily bread.
Forgive us our sins
as we forgive those who sin against us.
Lead us not into temptation
But deliver us from evil.
For the kingdom, the power,
And the glory are yours
Now and for ever.
Amen.[1]

- Listen to 'The Lord's Prayer' on the *Open to God* cassette.

- In that prayer, we prayed, *'Forgive us our sins as we forgive those who sin against us'*

- The dying Lord Jesus cried from the cross: *'Father, forgive them, they do not know what they do'*

- The risen Lord Jesus claimed that if we forgive someone their sins they are gone for good

Is there anyone you need to forgive today? If so, pick up the stone that you brought with you to the meeting and, when you feel ready to drop any bitterness or resentment or jealousy or finger-pointing or other negative feelings towards that person, drop your stone. Let its 'plop' symbolise your desire to let go of emotions that have been festering inside you. Hear the *'Well done!'* whispered by the Risen One.

If you find yourself struggling to let go but are unable to do so at this moment in time because the memories that surface are too painful, gaze at the picture of the Risen Lord Jesus on page 83. Notice how he is in close touch with God the Father (symbolised by the hands reaching down from heaven) and with the Holy Spirit (the dove). Ask God the

---

1. The Lord's Prayer, *Common Worship*, London, Church House Publishing, 2000, p. 44.

Father, the Son and the Holy Spirit to come into your hurt and to heal the pain. This may not happen immediately. It can happen, though, over a period of time so open yourself to a healing touch from the Risen One. Ask him, too, to help you to be willing to be made willing to forgive when the time is ripe. This is a prayer God honours and delights in – so, if you have been able to pray in this way, drop your stone when you are ready.

When the stones have been dropped, say together the following prayer:

Come Risen Lord Jesus
'Easter in us,
be a day-spring to the dimness of us'[1]
today
and
always
that we may bring glory to you.

• The risen, triumphant Lord Jesus entered the locked room where his disciples were hiding on the first Easter evening and he greeted them with one word, *'Shalom!'* – *Peace*. Calling each person by name, greet one another now with a sign of peace: like a smile, a touch, a handshake, a hug and with the words *'Peace be with you _____'*

---

1. The first two lines are well-known, well-loved words penned by Gerard Manley Hopkins, SJ, and first appeared in his poem *The Wreck of the Deutschland*.

Epilogue

After the Resurrection, as we have seen, the disciples faced the challenge of adjusting to a new way of relating to Jesus. Before his Crucifixion, these men had been with Jesus almost every day. They literally walked with him and talked with him, ate with him, slept near him, learned from him. Now they discovered that there were times when Jesus appeared and made himself known to them. There were other times when, although he was attentive to their needs, they could neither see nor hear him. This change in the dynamic of their relationship presented them with a huge challenge of trust.

The challenge that faces us as we journey on is not dissimilar. Like the disciples we need to recognise that, wherever we are, whatever we are doing, Jesus is with us. We shall not always see him or feel him, sense him or hear him yet we can trust that he is there because he has promised never to leave us or forsake us. Our privilege in life, then, is to do everything we need to do as though we were doing it for God and in his presence. Another challenge we face is to try to learn the art of seeing and sensing and hearing God wherever we are – at work, in the city, in the country-side, at home – literally everywhere. This is comparatively easy when we go on the kind of retreat I described in the Introduction to this book. As I described it on one such Easter retreat:

> I saw you in the fullness of the moon
> that lighted my path
> on the way to the tomb.

> I saw you in the dove-shaped cloud
> that hovered over the hills
> as we waited for the sun to rise.

> I saw you in the sun that
> slid over the mountain
> in all its majesty
> thrilling us with its appearance.

> I saw you in the liquid gold cross
> traced on the sea
> by the rays of the rising sun.

I worshipped you
in the strains of the aria from Handel's *Messiah*
that heralded the sunrise:
'I know that my Redeemer liveth . . .'

I heard and felt you when,
like the angel,
I sat outside the garden tomb
and wanted to shriek:
'He is not here . . . he is risen.'

Joy, pure joy.

Seeing and sensing God's nearness and dearness is not so easy when life is hectic so the greater challenge is to carry this openness, this trust, this sense of expectation into the mundane of the everyday. A prayer penned by St Clare, though, reminds us that the Risen One *will* make his presence known from now into eternity:

May the Risen One
be with you
always
and may you be with
HIM
always
and everywhere.

---

1. An adaptation of a blessing of St Clare.